Informing the legislative debate since 1914 _____

The Doctrine of Constitutional Avoidance: A Legal Overview

Andrew Nolan
Legislative Attorney

September 2, 2014

Congressional Research Service

7-5700

www.crs.gov

R43706

Summary

Article III of the Constitution established the judicial branch of the United States, staffing the branch with life-tenured and salary-protected judges. Amongst the powers of the federal judiciary is the power of "judicial review"—that is, the power to invalidate the acts of other branches of government and the states that contravene the Constitution. The Framers of the Constitution established this "countermajoritarian" role for the judiciary to help protect the written Constitution and its principles against incursions from the political branches. The power of judicial review is both a potent and controversial power, as American history has been replete with examples of outcry at when unelected federal judges invalidate the acts of a democratically elected branch of government. The potential for backlash to judicial review by the political branches has resulted in what late Professor Alexander Bickel termed a "countermajoritarian difficulty," as the judiciary is needed to protect the basic principles of the Constitution, but is also necessarily dependent on the political branches to enforce the judiciary's mandates. In other words, judicial review, while necessary to protect the mandates of the Constitution, is inherently antidemocratic, risking an erosion of the judiciary's role in the American constitutional form of government.

The prominent solution to the potential perils of the countermajoritarian difficulty, as espoused by Professor Bickel, is that the judiciary—and in particular the High Court—should exercise the "passive virtues," a set of tools, such as the justiciability doctrines, with which a court can return an unsettled and controversial constitutional problem to the political realm for resolution. The logic of Bickel's theory is that by "staying its hand" a court can avoid unnecessary entanglement in controversial and sensitive constitutional issues, while simultaneously allowing the judiciary to better gauge what is the appropriate constitutional principle animating a particular issue. Professor Bickel's work has been built on by Professor Cass Sunstein, who has argued that when the Supreme Court does reach the merits of a constitutional question (as opposed to avoiding the question entirely), the Court should practice "judicial minimalism,"—that is, in deciding cases, judges should say no more than necessary to justify an outcome and leave as much as possible undecided. Sunstein justified his theories on the grounds that minimalism reduces burdens on the Supreme Court and promotes democratic dialogue on difficult constitutional law questions.

The works of Professors Bickel and Sunstein are anchored in "deeply rooted" precedent from the Supreme Court in a doctrine called the constitutional avoidance doctrine. The doctrine was perhaps best articulated in a concurrence by Justice Louis Brandeis in *Ashwander v. TVA*, in which Justice Brandeis listed seven different loosely related rules that allow a court to avoid issuing broad rulings on matters of constitutional law. A host of recent cases from the Roberts Court on some of the most controversial legal issues currently facing the nation—including foreign surveillance, gay marriage, voting rights, the scope of Congress's enumerated powers, affirmative action, and mandatory union dues—have deployed the *Ashwander* rules to avoid having the Supreme Court issue broad rulings on the Constitution. After providing general background on the power of judicial review and the major theories on the constitutional avoidance doctrine, this report explores the various rules that allow a court to avoid a ruling that invalidates a democratically enacted law and the logic behind those rules. The report concludes with an exploration of how the doctrine of constitutional avoidance has influenced some of the recent jurisprudence of the Roberts Court, criticisms of the doctrine, and the implications for Congress.

Contents

Tables

Contacts

Introduction

Article III of the Constitution established the judicial branch of the United States, consisting of the Supreme Court and of any "inferior Courts as the Congress may from time to time ordain and establish...."[1] To staff such courts, the Constitution empowered life-tenured and salary-protected judges to adjudicate certain "cases" or "controversies," including cases arising under the Constitution.[2] The Supreme Court, in *Marbury v. Madison,* held that the judicial power to interpret the Constitution necessarily includes the power of judicial review[3]—that is, the power to countermand the decisions by other government agents because a given decision contravenes the Constitution.[4] Judicial review is not only a potent tool for the judiciary—it is also a controversial one, in that unelected federal judges possess the power to undo the decisions of the branches that are theoretically the most responsive to the people. From the early days of the republic to the New Deal to modern times, the history of the United States is replete with examples of conflicts between the political branches and the judiciary over the latter's use of the power of judicial review.[5] Indeed, over the last two terms of the Supreme Court, the High Court, whether in striking down Section 3 of the federal Defense of Marriage Act (DOMA) in *United States v. Windsor*[6] or Section 441 of the Federal Election Campaign Act (FECA) in *McCutcheon v. FEC,*[7] has shown a willingness to exercise its power to invalidate a congressionally enacted law, and, in turn, the Supreme Court's exercise of the power of judicial review has led to sharp criticisms of the Court and accusations of judicial "activism" thwarting the will of the majority.[8]

---

[1] *See* U.S. CONST. art. III, § 1.

[2] *Id.* art. III, § 2.

[3] 5 U.S. (1 Cranch) 137, 178 (1803) ("If then the courts are to regard the constitution; and the constitution is superior to any ordinary act of the legislature; the constitution, and not such ordinary act, must govern the case to which they both apply.").

[4] *See* Black's Law Dictionary (9th ed. 2009) (defining "judicial review" as a "court's power to review the actions of other branches or levels of government; esp., the courts' power to invalidate legislative and executive actions as being unconstitutional.").

[5] *See infra "Judicial Review and the Countermajoritarian Difficulty."*

[6] *See* 570 U.S. __, 133 S. Ct. 2675 (2013).

[7] *See* 572 U.S. __, 134 S. Ct. 1434 (2014).

[8] For examples of criticisms of the *Windsor* decision and the role of judicial review, *see, e.g.,* Former Governor Mike Huckabee, as quoted in Jeff Poor, *Huckabee on Supreme Court gay marriage ruling: 'Jesus wept,'* DAILY CALLER, (June 26, 2013), http://dailycaller.com/2013/06/26/huckabee-on-supreme-court-gay-marriage-ruling-jesus-wept/ ("Five people in robes said they are bigger than the voters of California and Congress combined."); Senator Lindsey Graham, as quoted in Kate Nocera, *Supreme Court Rulings Reveal Republican Rift on Marriage Equality,* BUZZFEED NEWS (June 26, 2013), http://www.buzzfeed.com/katenocera/supreme-court-rulings-reveal-republican-rift-on-marriage-equ#wwpzpu ("In my view elected officials should be defining marriage, not judges, but the court has ruled and I respect the court."); *but see* Senator Harry Reid, *Reid Statement on the Supreme Court's Decision for Marriage Equality,* press release, (June 26, 2013), http://www.reid.senate.gov/press_releases/reid-statement-on-the-supreme-courts-decision-for-marriage-equality#.U_yHH4UUqSo ("I'm glad that today the Supreme Court recognized that the federal government has no business picking and choosing which American couples get the legal recognition and protections they deserve."). For examples of criticisms of the *McCutcheon* decision and the role of judicial review, *see, e.g.,* Senator Tammy Baldwin, *Baldwin's statement on Supreme Court Decision in McCutcheon v. Federal Election Commission,* press release, (April 2, 2014), http://www.baldwin.senate.gov/blog/baldwins-statement-on-supreme-court-decision-in-mccutcheon-v-federal-election-commission ("This decision is extremely disappointing but not surprising coming from an activist court majority that has previously opened the floodgates of corporate special interest influence in our elections with the Citizens United decision."); Senator Bernie Sanders, *Supreme Court Voids Campaign Spending Limits,* press release, (April 2, 2014), http://www.sanders.senate.gov/newsroom/press-releases/supreme-
(continued...)

Notwithstanding the recent high-profile matters in which the Court has exercised its often controversial power of judicial review, judicial invalidation of democratically enacted laws on constitutional grounds remains relatively rare at the Supreme Court. Of the 75 opinions issued by the Roberts Court in the October 2013 term, only one decision—*McCutcheon*—invalidated a congressionally enacted law on constitutional grounds,[9] and three cases[10] declared a positive enactment under state law to be unconstitutional.[11] The Court's apparent reticence in using judicial review is supported by long-standing case law cautioning against judicial review and counseling courts to "avoid" unnecessarily broad rulings on constitutional questions. For example, the Supreme Court has established a "time-honored presumption" that a congressionally enacted law is constitutional,[12] and, as a general rule, courts should not "pass on questions of constitutionality ... unless such adjudication is unavoidable."[13] Indeed, the Supreme Court has established a host of loosely related rules generally called the constitutional avoidance doctrine that discourage a federal court from issuing broad rulings on matters of constitutional law.[14] After providing general background on the power of judicial review and the major theories justifying the constitutional avoidance doctrine, this report explores the various rules that allow a court to avoid a broad ruling that invalidates a democratically enacted law and the logic behind those rules. The report concludes with an exploration of how the doctrine of constitutional avoidance has influenced some of the recent jurisprudence of the Roberts Court, criticisms of the doctrine, and the implications for Congress.

Judicial Review and the Countermajoritarian Difficulty

In establishing the federal tripartite government, the Framers of the Constitution, while proponents of democracy,[15] were wary of any form of unchecked power, even when that power

---

(...continued)

court-voids-campaign-spending-limits ("What world are the five conservative Supreme Court justices living in? ... To equate the ability of billionaires to buy elections with 'freedom of speech' is totally absurd."); *but see* Senator Mitch McConnell, *McConnell Statement on Supreme Court Decision in* McCutcheon v. FEC, press release, (April 2, 2014), http://www.mcconnell.senate.gov/public/index.cfm?p=PressReleases&ContentRecord_id=57f6000c-f6a3-44e1-af0c-e900b087d0a4 ("[T]he court did recognize that it is the right of the individual, and not the prerogative of Congress, to determine how many candidates and parties to support.").

[9] Other cases invalidated discrete executive actions on constitutional grounds. *See, e.g.,* NLRB v. Noel Canning, 573 U.S. __, 134 S. Ct. 2550 (2014) (concluding that the President lacked the power to make recess appointments during a three-day recess amidst a *pro forma* session of Congress).

[10] *See* Harris v. Quinn, 573 U.S. __, 134 S. Ct. 896 (2014) (striking down the Illinois Public Labor Relations Act as applied to "personal assistants" that provide homecare services); McCullen v. Coakley, 573 U.S. __, 134 S. Ct. 2518 (2014) (striking down the Massachusetts Reproductive Health Care Facilities Act); Hall v. Florida, 572 U.S. __, 134 S. Ct. 1986 (2014) (striking down Fla. Stat. § 921.137).

[11] The Court in other cases applied the Constitution to invalidate discrete actions or practices by state officials, *see, e.g.,* California v. Riley, 573 U.S. __, 134 S. Ct. 2473 (2014) (holding that the search of the contents of a cell phone during an arrest violated the Fourth Amendment), or state common law as interpreted by a state court, *see, e.g.,* Northwest Inc. v. Ginsberg, 572 U.S. __, 134 S. Ct. 1422 (2014) (holding that the Airline Deregulation Act, together with the Supremacy Clause of the Constitution, preempts a state law claim for breach of the implied covenant of good faith and fair dealing).

[12] *See* Reno v. Condon, 528 U.S. 141, 148 (2000).

[13] *See* Spector Motor Service, Inc., McLaughlin, 323 U.S. 101, 105 (1944).

[14] *See infra "The "Passive Virtues" and Judicial Minimalism."*

[15] *See* The Federalist, No. 49, at 281-82 (James Madison) (Clinton Rossiter ed., 1999) ("[T]he people are the only (continued...)

---

was lodged in a democratic majority.[16] As a consequence, the Framers envisioned a written Constitution, which protected specific values, principles, and rights, as a limit of what could be changed through ordinary political processes.[17] Because the political branches may not be expected to always adhere to the constitutional limitations placed on each body, as these branches are most directly responsive to the often temporary whims of the people, the federal judiciary established under Article III was deliberately designed by the Framers of the Constitution to be a "countermajoritarian" branch that interpreted the written Constitution and protected its principles.[18] The Constitution did this by "insulating the federal judiciary" from potential pressures, from either the political branches or the public, which could potentially "skew the decision making process or compromise the integrity or legitimacy of federal court decisions."[19] The key sources of the judiciary "insulation" from the political processes are the Good Behavior Clause and the Compensation Clause of Article III. For the Framers, the Good Behavior Clause, by creating a "permanent tenure of judicial offices," ensures an "independent spirit in judges,"[20] and the Compensation Clause, by creating a "fixed provision for [the judiciary's] support," prevents the political branches from having power over a judge's subsistence and, with that, "power over his will."[21] While the Constitution itself is silent on the power of judicial review, in *Marbury v. Madison,* Chief Justice John Marshall formally concluded that the logic of the written Constitution coupled with an independent judiciary necessitated the federal judiciary's unique role in being able to invalidate the acts of other branches of government that contravened the Constitution.[22]

In contrast to the political branches, the federal judiciary as envisioned by the nation's founding document arguably raised few concerns and was the subject of little debate for the Framers of the Constitution.[23] Records from the Constitutional Convention of 1787 consist of "surprisingly little" on the federal judiciary.[24] Most delegates to the Convention took "for granted" even the

---

(...continued)

legitimate fountain of power, and it is from them that the constitutional charter ... is derived.... ").

[16] Martin H. Redish and Karen L. Drizin, *Constitutional Federalism and Judicial Review: The Role of Textual Analysis,* 62 N.Y.U.L. REV. 1, 15 (1987); *see also* THE FEDERALIST, No. 49, at 285 (James Madison) (Clinton Rossiter ed., 1999) ("But it is the reason, alone, of the public, that ought to control and regulate the government. The passions ought to be controlled and regulated by the government.")

[17] *See* Redish and Drizin, *supra* note 16, at 15. Alexander Hamilton, in Federalist No. 78, envisioned a "limited Constitution" that "contains certain specified exceptions" to a given branch's power—such as the prohibition on the legislature's ability to enact bills of attainder or *ex post facto* laws. *See* THE FEDERALIST, No. 78, at 434 (Alexander Hamilton) (Clinton Rossiter ed., 1999).

[18] *See* THE FEDERALIST, No. 78, at 435 (Alexander Hamilton) (Clinton Rossiter ed., 1999) ("[C]ourts were designed to be an intermediate body between the people and the legislature in order ... to keep the latter within the limits assigned to their authority."); *see generally* ALEXANDER M. BICKEL, THE LEAST DANGEROUS BRANCH: THE SUPREME COURT AT THE BAR OF POLITICS 16-17 (1962).

[19] Martin H. Redish, *Federal Judicial Independence: Constitutional and Political Perspectives,* 46 MERCER L. REV. 697, 700-701 (1995).

[20] *See* THE FEDERALIST, No. 78, at 437 (Alexander Hamilton) (Clinton Rossiter ed., 1999).

[21] *See* THE FEDERALIST, No. 79, at 440 (Alexander Hamilton) (Clinton Rossiter ed., 1999).

[22] *See* 5 U.S. (1 Cranch) 137, 177-78 (1803); *see generally* Michael Stokes Paulsen, *The Irrepressible Myth of Marbury,* 101 MICH. L. REV. 2706, 2707 (2003) (criticizing the widely-held belief that judicial review was established by *Marbury* and instead pointing out that *Marbury* merely applied well-established principles respecting the Court's powers).

[23] *See* Richard H. Fallon, Jr. et al., HART AND WECHSLER'S THE FEDERAL COURTS AND THE FEDERAL SYSTEM 1 (5th ed. 2003) ("For most of the delegates, the judiciary was a secondary or even a tertiary concern.").

[24] Max Farrand, THE RECORDS OF THE FEDERAL CONVENTION 154 (1911) (noting that for "[o]ne who is especially (continued...)

---

seemingly most controversial aspect of the federal judicial power, the power of judicial review.[25] Moreover, the Constitution itself devotes—relative to the other branches—very little attention to the role of the judiciary: less than 500 words.[26] And in the midst of the debate over whether to ratify the Constitution, Alexander Hamilton famously downplayed anti-federalist concerns regarding the power of the federal courts, calling the judiciary the "least dangerous branch" because the judiciary possesses neither the power of the purse, like the legislative branch, nor the power of the sword, like the executive branch.[27]

In sharp contrast to the views of the Framers, American history has been replete with examples of outcry at the scope of the powers provided to the unelected federal judiciary. Thomas Jefferson, in the wake of his presidency, disavowed the power of judicial review, arguing that "[e]ach of the three departments has equally the right to decide for itself what is its duty under the constitution, without any regard to what the others may have decided for themselves under a similar question."[28] Andrew Jackson, in vetoing the reauthorization of the Bank of the United States, dismissed the 1819 case *McCulloch v. Maryland* that upheld the constitutionality of the Bank,[29] contending that "the opinion of the judges has no more authority over Congress than the opinion of Congress has over the judges, and on that point the President is independent of both."[30] In the wake of *Dred Scott v. Sandford* and its declaration that African Americans had "no rights which the white man was bound to respect,"[31] Abraham Lincoln, in his first inaugural address, famously noted that,

> if the policy of government upon vital questions ... is to be irrevocably fixed by decisions of the Supreme Court ... the people will have ceased to be their own rulers, having ... practically resigned their government into the hands of that eminent tribunal.[32]

While modern criticisms of the Court have eschewed explicitly disputing *Marbury*'s central holding, controversies over the power of judicial review have extended into the 20th and 21st centuries. In 1935, Franklin Roosevelt prepared a message announcing that he would ignore the Court's decision in the *Gold Clause Cases*,[33] deterred only by a favorable ruling by the High

---

(...continued)

interested in the judiciary, there is surprisingly little on the subject to be found in the records of the convention.").

[25] *See* Fallon, *supra* note 23, at 11; *see also* Saikrishna B. Prakash & John C. Yoo, *The Origins of Judicial Review*, 70 U. CHI. L. REV. 887, 951-53 (2003) (arguing that historical evidence indicates that "[n]umerous delegates ... foresaw that judicial review would arise from a written, limited constitution with a separation of powers."); *but see* Larry D. Kramer, *Foreword: We the Court*, 115 HARV. L. REV. 4, 64 (2001) (arguing that only a few delegates expressed any views on judicial review at the Convention and the framers did not endorse a robust vision of judicial review).

[26] *See* U.S. CONST. art. III; *see also* G. Brinton Lucas, *Structural Exceptionalism and Comparative Constitutional Law*, 96 VA. L. REV. 1965, 1978 (2010) ("Article III of the U.S. Constitution is striking in its brevity. Less than five hundred words long, the Constitution's treatment of the federal judiciary pales in comparison to its detailed discussions of the legislative and executive branches.").

[27] *See* THE FEDERALIST, No. 78, at 433 (Alexander Hamilton) (Clinton Rossiter ed., 1999).

[28] *See Letter from Thomas Jefferson to Spencer Roane* (Sept. 6, 1819), in 10 THE WRITINGS OF THOMAS JEFFERSON 1816-1826, at 140 (Paul Leicester Ford ed., New York, G.P. Putnam's Sons 1899).

[29] 17 U.S. 316 (1819).

[30] *See* Andrew Jackson, *Veto Message* (July 10, 1832), *available at* http://avalon.law.yale.edu/19th_century/ajveto01.asp.

[31] 60 U.S. 393, 19 How. 393, 406, 407, 15 L. Ed. 691 (1857).

[32] *See* Abraham Lincoln, *First Inaugural Address of Abraham Lincoln,* (Mar. 4, 1861), *available at* http://avalon.law.yale.edu/19th_century/lincoln1.asp.

[33] *See* Kathleen M. Sullivan & Gerald Gunther, CONSTITUTIONAL LAW 24-25 (16th ed. 2005) (discussing Franklin
(continued...)

Court.[34] And the Supreme Court's invalidation of several of the central features of Roosevelt's New Deal[35] spurred the President's infamous "court packing" plan aimed at limiting the power of the Court to invalidate progressive legislation.[36] Two decades later, the Court's decision in *Brown vs. Board of Education* ending racial segregation in public schools[37] spurred intense backlash against the Court in the South, with one prominent southern Senator going so far as to describe *Brown* as a "legislative decision by a political court.... "[38] By the late 1960s, Richard Nixon coined the phrase "judicial activism" to describe the constitutional jurisprudence of the Warren Court and pledged to appoint "strict constructionists" to the Court to "restore" a proper "balance,"[39] leading some scholars to suggest that Nixon's message in 1968 was centered on the anti-*Marbury* proposition that it was "not for the Court to be deciding major constitutional issues."[40] And President Obama, following oral argument regarding the constitutionality of the Affordable Care Act, expressed concern that an "unelected group of people" would take the "unprecedented, extraordinary step of overturning a law that was passed by a strong majority of a democratically elected Congress."[41]

The Framers' treatment of the judiciary's powers juxtaposed with the political branches' often-fractious relationship with the judiciary illustrates the "root difficulty" with the power of judicial review.[42] On one hand, an independent judiciary is needed to ensure that the core norms of our society, as embodied in the Constitution, are enforced against temporary populist interests.[43] After all, according to Professor Alexander Bickel in his seminal work *The Least Dangerous Branch*, "when the pressure for immediate results is strong enough and emotions ride high enough," the political branches may "prefer to act on expediency rather than take the long view."[44] In contrast to acting on "expediency," the federal judiciary, per Bickel, acts on "principle"[45] and, therefore, should be expected to be the central governmental actor that, for example, enforces the First Amendment to "protect unpopular individuals from retaliation—and their ideas from

---

(...continued)

Roosevelt's proposed gold clause speech).

[34] *See* Norman v. Baltimore & Ohio R.R., 294 U.S. 240 (1935) and Perry v. United States, 294 U.S. 330 (1935).

[35] *See, e.g.,* Schechter Poultry Corp. v. United States, 295 U.S. 495 (1935) (striking down the National Industrial Recovery Act); Carter v. Carter Coal Co., 293 U.S. 388 (1935) (invalidating the Bituminous Coal Act).

[36] *See generally* Jeffrey Shesol, Supreme Power: Franklin Roosevelt vs. the Supreme Court 243-250 (2010).

[37] 347 U.S. 483 (1954).

[38] *See* Senator James Eastland, as quoted by Lucas A. Powe, Jr., The Warren Court and American Politics 218 (2000).

[39] *See* Richard Nixon, *Remarks on Accepting the Presidential Nomination of the Republican National Convention* (Aug. 8, 1968), available at http://www.presidency.ucsb.edu/ws/index.php?pid=3537#axzz1lSqYLW00.

[40] *See* David Fontana and Donald Braman, *Judicial Backlash? Evidence From a National Experiment,* 112 Colum. L. Rev. 731, 741 (2012).

[41] *See* Barack Obama as quoted by Jeff Mason, *Obama Takes a Shot at Supreme Court Over Healthcare,* Reuters (Apr. 2, 2012), http://www.reuters.com/article/2012/04/02/us-obama-healthcare-idUSBRE8310WP20120402.

[42] *See* Bickel, *supra* note 18, at 16 ("The root difficulty is that judicial review is a counter-majoritarian force in our system.").

[43] *Id.* at 17 ("[D]ecisions that have been submitted to the electoral process ... are not continually resubmitted, and they are certainly not continually unmade. Once run through the process, once rendered by "the people," ... myriad decisions remain to govern the present and future despite what may well be fluctuating majorities against them at any given time.").

[44] *Id.* at 25.

[45] *Id.*

---

suppression—at the hand of an intolerant society."[46] And when the Court opts to shirk its duty to act on "principle" and instead upholds a law that may not in actuality adhere to core constitutional norms, the High Court "legitimates" or validates that law, and, in so doing, risks damage to the basic values undergirding our system of government.[47]

On the other hand, when a court "declares unconstitutional a legislative act or the action of an elected executive, [the court] thwarts" the enforcement of an act that presumably reflects the will of the voters.[48] As a result, judicial review necessarily invites conflict with the political branches. This "countermajoritarian difficulty"[49]—a phrase coined by Professor Bickel—creates a fundamental dilemma for a court, because the judiciary, lacking either the power of the "sword" or "purse,"[50] cannot enforce its own decisions and must rely on external support to "compel recalcitrant parties" to comply with a given ruling.[51] As a consequence, the "Court's power lies ... in its legitimacy, a product of substance and perception that shows itself in the people's acceptance of the Judiciary as fit to determine what the Nation's law means and to declare what it demands."[52] In turn, a Court that is overly aggressive in its exercise of judicial review or simply abuses that power risks losing its legitimacy and, with that, invites political and cultural backlash that can undermine the role of the judiciary in our system of government.[53] More broadly, aggressive use of judicial review can "seriously ... weaken the democratic process."[54] After all, by striking down legislation on a constitutional ground a court not only voids the law that is being challenged, but generally prohibits *any* future version of that law from being enacted. And if a court's act of judicial review is simply mistaken or proves to be unwise, the constitutional nature of a decision forecloses a legislature from correcting the error. As a result, at its worst, judicial review can "foreclos[e] all democratic outlet for the deep passions" on a particular issue and invite intense conflict within the nation.[55] Given the challenges posed by the countermajoritarian difficulty, ultimately the question for the Supreme Court is how to maintain the "peaceful coexistence of the countermajoritarian implications of judicial review and the democratic principles upon which our Federal Government ... rests."[56]

The "Passive Virtues" and Judicial Minimalism

In *The Least Dangerous Branch*, Professor Alexander Bickel proposed a solution to the countermajoritarian difficulty, a solution that has deep roots in the High Court's constitutional jurisprudence and has been the inspiration for many members of the judiciary when approaching

---

[46] McIntyre v. Ohio Elections Comm'n, 514 U.S. 334, 357 (1995).

[47] *See* Bickel, *supra* note 18, at 129-30.

[48] *Id.* at 16-17.

[49] *Id.* at 16.

[50] *See* THE FEDERALIST, No. 78, at 435 (Alexander Hamilton) (Clinton Rossiter ed., 1999).

[51] *See* Michael J. Klarman, *The Plessy Era*, 1998 Sup. Ct. Rev. 303, 392 (1998).

[52] Planned Parenthood v. Casey, 505 U.S. 833, 865 (1992) (plurality opinion).

[53] *See generally* Gerald N. Rosenberg, THE HOLLOW HOPE, CAN COURTS BRING ABOUT SOCIAL CHANGE? (1991); Mark V. Tushnet, TAKING THE CONSTITUTION AWAY FROM THE COURTS (2000).

[54] *See* Bickel, *supra* note 18, at 21.

[55] *See Casey*, 505 U.S. 833, 1002 (Scalia, J., dissenting) (citing the example of *Dred Scott* and its role in bringing about the American Civil War to demonstrate the dangers of unprincipled judicial review).

[56] *See* United States v. Richardson, 418 U.S. 166, 192 (Powell, J., concurring).

difficult constitutional questions. Bickel argued that when the Supreme Court is faced with a difficult question of constitutional law, the Court need not as a matter of course exercise the power of judicial review and serve in either a legitimating or countermajoritarian role.[57] Instead of validating a law or striking down a piece of legislation, Bickel noted that the Court "*may do neither*" and simply "stay[] its hand."[58]

The Supreme Court can opt for the third route by practicing the so-called "passive virtues," a set of tools, such as the justiciability doctrines and the Court's discretionary *certiorari* power, with which the Court can return an unsettled constitutional problem to the political realm for resolution.[59] For Bickel, by employing the "passive virtues" and exercising judicial review only when constitutional principles are sufficiently clear for resolution, the Court can avoid unnecessary entanglement in controversial and sensitive constitutional issues, protecting the judiciary from potential backlash by the political branches and preserving the Court's role as the protector of established constitutional principles.[60] At the same time, the use of the "passive virtues," according to Bickel, encourages constitutional dialogue within the other branches and the public and allows the Court to better gauge what is the appropriate constitutional principle animating a particular issue.[61] Put another way, for Professor Bickel, the value of the "passive virtues" can be summarized in a short quote from Justice Louis Brandeis: "The most important thing we do is not doing."[62]

Professor Cass Sunstein's work on "judicial minimalism" is often seen as the modern continuation of Professor Bickel's work.[63] In contrast to Bickel's focus on a court's silence in response to a controversial constitutional question, however, Sunstein's approach to constitutional adjudication is geared toward the type of response the Supreme Court should provide when it reaches the merits of the constitutional question that has been presented to the Court.[64] Specifically, Professor Sunstein advocates for "judicial minimalism"—that is, in deciding cases, judges should "say[] no more than necessary to justify an outcome, and leav[e] as much as possible undecided.... "[65] In particular, courts, according to Sunstein, should strive to make rulings that are both narrow—decisions that are no broader than necessary to resolve the case at hand[66]—and shallow—decisions that avoid questions of basic principle and reach "concrete judgments on particular cases, unaccompanied by abstract accounts about what accounts for those judgments."[67]

---

[57] *See* Bickel, *supra* note 18, at 69.

[58] *Id.* at 69-70.

[59] *Id.* at 111; *see generally* Alexander M. Bickel, *Foreword: The Passive Virtues*, 75 HARV. L. REV. 40 (1961).

[60] *See* Bickel, *supra* note 18, at 70.

[61] *Id.* at 115.

[62] *Id.* at 71, 112.

[63] *See, e.g.,* Catherine Bateup, *The Dialogic Promise. Assessing the Normative Potential of Theories of Constitutional Dialogue,* 71 BROOK. L. REV. 1109, 1131-35 (2006).

[64] *See* Cass R. Sunstein, ONE CASE AT A TIME: JUDICIAL MINIMALISM ON THE SUPREME COURT 3 (1999).

[65] *Id.*

[66] *Id.* at 10-11.

[67] *Id.* at 13. In this sense, Sunstein's focus on "shallow" rulings that do not rely on basic principles sets his theories apart from those of Bickel, who deeply relied on the notion of principle guiding the Court's rulings. *See* Jonathan T. Molot, *Principled Minimalism: Restriking the Balance Between Judicial Minimalism and Neutral Principles,* 90 VA. L. REV. 1753, 1779 (2004) ("Sunstein seems to accept principle grudgingly, rather than to embrace it as part of the solution to the countermajoritarian difficulty. Too much principle would foreclose too many options in his view, and so (continued...)

Sunstein, echoing Bickel, justifies his theory of minimalism on two separate grounds. First, Professor Sunstein argues that minimalism reduces burdens on the judiciary in trying to reach a decision.[68] For Sunstein, at least with respect to the Supreme Court, attempting to wholly resolve a broad and complex constitutional legal issue by a "multimember court, consisting of diverse people who disagree on a great deal," in a single opinion may be time-consuming, resource-draining, and poorly suited to the competencies of the Court.[69] Second, and perhaps most important to Sunstein, minimalism makes "judicial errors less frequent and (above all) less damaging," as a court that "leaves things open will not foreclose options in a way that may do a great deal of harm."[70] As a consequence, Sunstein views judicial minimalism to go hand-in-hand with democratic deliberation, as minimalist rulings on major constitutional issues "increase the space for further reflection and debate at the local, state, and national levels, simply because [such rulings] do not foreclose subsequent decisions."[71] In this sense, like Bickel, Sunstein proposes a judicial philosophy aimed at successfully responding to the "countermajoritarian difficulty."[72]

The *Ashwander* Doctrine

Professor Bickel's "passive virtues," Professor Sunstein's "minimalism," and the general theories of constitutional avoidance are not grounded purely in theory, but instead have their basis in long-standing Supreme Court case law. As Justice Felix Frankfurter wrote over 70 years ago, "[i]f there is one doctrine more deeply rooted than any other in the process of constitutional adjudication, it is that we ought not pass on questions of constitutionality ... unless such adjudication is unavoidable."[73] To understand the modern influence of constitutional avoidance on judicial decision making, the starting point is the most famous articulation[74] of the constitutional avoidance doctrine and the various "passive virtues": Justice Brandeis's concurring opinion in *Ashwander v. Tennessee Valley Authority (TVA).*[75]

Ashwander v. TVA and Brandeis's Concurrence

In *Ashwander,* George Ashwander and other preferred shareholders of the Alabama Power Company, after unsuccessfully petitioning the company, sued the corporation and the TVA over a contract between the government agency and the power company.[76] Specifically, the plaintiffs challenged the legality of a contract that the company had entered into with the government

---

(...continued)

principle should be kept to a minimum.").

[68] *See* Sunstein, *supra* note 64, at 4.

[69] *Id.*

[70] *Id.*

[71] *Id.*

[72] *See* Christine Bateup, *The Dialogic Promise Assessing The Normative Potential of Theories of Constitutional Dialogue,* 71 Brooklyn L. Rev. 1109, 1133 (2006) (arguing that "judicial minimalism is quite successful in responding to the countermajoritarian difficulty.").

[73] Spector Motor Service, Inc. v. McLaughlin, 323 U.S. 101, 103 (1944).

[74] *See* Lisa A. Kloppenberg, *Avoiding Constitutional Questions,* 35 B.C. L. Rev. 1003, 1012 (1994) (describing Brandeis's concurrence as "the most significant formulation of the avoidance doctrine.").

[75] 297 U.S. 288, 345-48 (Brandeis, J., concurring) (1936).

[76] 297 U.S. 288, 316-17 (1936) (plurality opinion).

agency to (1) purchase the company's property and transmission facilities and (2) sell the company surplus power generated by the government-owned Wilson Dam in northern Alabama.[77] Among the legal theories espoused by the plaintiffs was that the TVA acted in excess of the federal government's constitutional authority when it entered into the contract.[78] A plurality opinion, written by Chief Justice Hughes, ruled against the plaintiffs, upholding Congress's constitutional authority to both construct the Wilson Dam and dispose of electric energy generated at the dam based on Congress's war power, the commerce power, and the power to dispose of property belonging to the United States.[79]

In an opinion epitomizing Professor Bickel's advocacy for the "passive virtues," Justice Brandeis, joined by three other Justices, wrote a concurring opinion in which he argued that while he agreed with the Court's resolution of the constitutional questions posed by the case, the constitutional questions in *Ashwander* should have been avoided by the Court.[80] Specifically, Brandeis argued that because the plaintiffs had already unsuccessfully voiced their complaints to the corporation, the plaintiffs had no "right to interfere" in corporate governance under the substantive law and, therefore, lacked a sufficient injury necessary to bring the lawsuit.[81] In addition, the concurrence noted that the stockholders could not show an "irreparable injury" to the plaintiffs' own property rights that would result from the allegedly illegal conduct of the government.[82] Finally, Justice Brandeis argued that even if the plaintiffs did possess a sufficient injury to maintain the lawsuit, the Court, in its discretion, can simply "refuse an injunction unless the alleged invalidity [of the law establishing the TVA] is clear."[83]

Placing his views in a broader context, in perhaps the most famous and quoted aspect of the *Ashwander* concurrence,[84] Justice Brandeis listed a "series of rules under which [the Court] has avoided passing upon a large part of all the constitutional questions pressed upon it for decision."[85] The seven rules contained within Brandeis's *Ashwander* concurrence and their corresponding modern doctrines are listed in **Table 1**.

Table 1. The Seven Rules of *Ashwander*

Rule	Modern Doctrine
The Court will not pass upon the constitutionality of legislation in a friendly, non-adversary, proceeding	Rule Against Feigned or Collusive Lawsuits
The Court will not "anticipate a question of constitutional law in advance of the necessity of deciding it."	Ripeness

---

[77] *Id.*

[78] *Id.*

[79] *Id.* at 326-30.

[80] 297 U.S. 288, 345-48 (Brandeis, J., concurring).

[81] *Id.* at 341-44.

[82] *Id.* at 345.

[83] *Id.* at 354.

[84] According to KeyCite search on Westlaw, as of late August 2014, Brandeis's *Ashwander* concurrence has been cited in 1,279 federal cases. A similar "FOCUS" search on LexisNexis showed that Brandeis's concurrence appeared in 1,265 federal cases.

[85] 297 U.S. 288, 346 (Brandeis, J., concurring).

Rule	Modern Doctrine
The Court will not "formulate a rule of constitutional law broader than is required by the precise facts to which it is to be applied."	Judicial Minimalism
The Court will not pass upon a constitutional question although properly presented by the record, if there is also present some other ground upon which the case may be disposed of.	Last Resort Rule
The Court will not pass upon the validity of a statute upon complaint of one who fails to show that he is injured by its operation.	Standing; Mootness
The Court will not pass upon the constitutionality of a statute at the instance of one who has availed himself of its benefits.	Constitutional Estoppel
When the validity of an act of the Congress is drawn in question, and even if a serious doubt of constitutionality is raised, it is a cardinal principle that this Court will first ascertain whether a construction of the statute is fairly possible by which the question may be avoided.	Constitutional Avoidance Canon

Source: *Ashwander v. TVA*, 297 U.S. 288, 345-48 (Brandeis, J., concurring) (1936).

It is important to note Justice Brandeis's rules and the entire avoidance doctrine are not unitary in nature, but rather consist of seven loosely related principles and canons that allow a court to avoid making broad rulings on constitutional grounds. Some of the *Ashwander* rules, such as the rule against feigned or collusive suits or the rule of constitutional estoppel, rarely arise in constitutional law litigation.[86] Moreover, other *Ashwander* rules have been largely subsumed by core Article III concerns, and to the extent a court dismisses a case based on a jurisdictional defect premised from a "principled interpretation[]" of Article III, the court would arguably not be acting solely out of a concern to "avoid" ruling on a constitutional question in line with the views of Justice Brandeis.[87] Nonetheless, the rules articulated by Justice Brandeis in his *Ashwander* concurrence form the basis for Professor Bickel's "passive virtues"[88] and Professor Sunstein's "minimalism"[89] and remain important tools used by federal courts to avoid making broad constitutional rulings.[90]

The Roberts Court and the *Ashwander Doctrine*

Perhaps the two most controversial opinions[91] issued by the Roberts Court are the Court's decisions in *Citizens United v. FEC,* respecting restrictions on corporate independent expenditures on political speech,[92] and *NFIB v. Sebelius,* regarding the constitutionality of the

---

[86] *See, e.g.* David P. Currie, *The Constitution in the Supreme Court,* 49 U. Chi. L. Rev. 887, 891 (1982) (noting the difficulty in proving a feigned or collusive case); Arnett v. Kennedy, 416 U.S. 134, 153 (1974) (noting that the doctrine of constitutional estoppel has "unquestionably been applied unevenly in the past, and observed as often as not in the breach.").

[87] *See* Fallon, *supra* note 23, at 86.

[88] *See* Bickel, *supra* note 18, at 115.

[89] *See* Cass R. Sunstein, *Foreword: Leaving Things Undecided,* 110 HARV. L. REV. 6, 51 (1996) (noting that "principles of justiciability - mootness, ripeness, reviewability, standing - can be understood as ways to minimize the judicial presence in American public life.").

[90] *See infra* "The Roberts Court and the *Ashwander* Doctrine."

[91] *See* Pamela Karlan, *The Supreme Court 2011 Term: Forward: Democracy and Disdain,* 126 HARV. L. REV. 1, 29 (2012) (arguing that "until *NFIB,* the most controversial decision of the Roberts Court was *Citizens United v. FEC.*").

[92] *See* Citizens United v. FEC, 558 U.S. 310 (2010).

Affordable Care Act's individual mandate and spending conditions imposed upon the states.[93] In both opinions, the Court opted to not issue a ruling on a non-constitutional ground, choosing instead to answer the broad constitutional questions posed in each case.[94] Critics of the decisions have accused the Court of "overreach" in each case,[95] and both cases have been cited by scholars as examples of the Roberts Court's alleged disdain for the perils of the countermajoritarian difficulty.[96]

While cases like *Citizens United* and *NFIB* certainly garner the attention of constitutional scholars and even the public, and while arguments can be made about the necessity of the scope of both of those rulings,[97] broad rulings on matters of constitutional law are a rarity at the Roberts Court. Indeed, the vast majority of opinions issued by the Supreme Court simply do not centrally involve a question of constitutional law.[98] Moreover, as will be discussed below, when the Supreme Court is squarely faced with a major constitutional question, the Roberts Court has frequently either avoided answering the question posed to it or resolved the constitutional question on narrow grounds,[99] illustrating the continued viability of the *Ashwander* doctrine.[100]

---

[93] *See* NFIB v. Sebelius, 132 S. Ct. 2566 (2012).

[94] *See Citizens United*, 558 U.S. at 329 ("It is not judicial restraint to accept an unsound, narrow argument just so the Court can avoid another argument with broader implications. Indeed, a court would be remiss in performing its duties were it to accept an unsound principle merely to avoid the necessity of making a broader ruling."); *see also NFIB*, 132 S. Ct. at 2584 (holding that the Anti-Injunction Act's restriction on the jurisdiction of the court applied, allowing the Court to "proceed to the merits" of the lawsuit).

[95] *See, e.g.*, Alliance for Justice, *The Roberts Court and Judicial Overreach*, 2013, 6-8 *available at* http://www.afj.org/wp-content/uploads/2013/09/the-roberts-court-and-judicial-overreach.pdf (highlighting *Citizens United* and *NFIB* as examples of "stealth judicial overreach"); Tonja Jacobi, *Obamacare as a Window on Judicial Strategy*, 80 Tenn. L. Rev. 763, 842 (2013) (arguing that Chief Justice Roberts's majority opinion in *NFIB* revealed "[Roberts] to be not a humble law applier, but a keen politico-legal strategist."); *but see Citizens United*, 558 U.S. at 374 (Roberts, C.J., concurring) (arguing that *Citizens United* "accords with our standard practice of avoiding broad constitutional questions except when necessary to decide the case before us."); and *NFIB*, 132 S. Ct. at 2579 ("Our permissive reading of these powers is explained in part by a general reticence to invalidate the acts of the Nation's elected leaders. 'Proper respect for a coordinate branch of the government' requires that we strike down an Act of Congress only if 'the lack of constitutional authority to pass [the] act in question is clearly demonstrated.") (internal citations omitted).

[96] *See* Karlan, *supra* note 91, at 57 (arguing the *NFIB* "issued a set of opinions that may set the terms of constitutional arguments for years to come," in sharp contrast to Bickel's passive virtues); *see also id.* at 29 (arguing that *Citizens United* elevated "a particular conception of liberty over the political branches' choice of a competing conception of equality."); *but see* Steven G. Calabresi, *The Constitution and Disdain*, 126 Harv. L. Rev. F. 13, 14-15, 19 (2012) (criticizing Professor Karlan's assessment of the countermajoritarian difficulty's applicability to *NFIB* and *Citizens United*).

[97] *See supra* notes 94-95.

[98] *See supra* notes 9-11 and accompanying text.

[99] The October 2013 term of the Supreme Court witnessed a remarkable uptick in the number of unanimous opinions. *See* Erwin Chemerinsky, *First impressions of this term's SCOTUS decisions were misleading*, ABA Journal, (Aug. 4, 2014), http://www.abajournal.com/news/article/chemerinsky_reexamining_this_terms_scotus_decisions_shows_initial_impressio/ ("A stunning 65 percent of the cases were decided unanimously, compared with 49 percent being unanimous in the term before and 43 percent being unanimous two years ago."). Some scholars contend that the recent unanimity trend may be due to the Court "not deciding the difficult, and likely divisive, issue presented, but instead resolving the case on narrow grounds." *Id.*

[100] Indeed, all but one Justice on the current Supreme Court has, at different times, cited to Brandeis' *Ashwander* concurrence for the proposition that judicial restraint requires the avoidance of broad constitutional rulings. *See* Bond v. United States, 134 S. Ct. 2077, 2087 (Roberts, C.J.); Camreta v. Greene, 131 S. Ct. 2020, 2031 (2011) (Kagan, J.); Stop the Beach Renourishment, Inc. v. Fla. Dep't of Envtl. Prot., 560 U.S. 702, 744 (2010) (Breyer, J., concurring); Pearson v. Callahan, 555 U.S. 223, 241 (2009) (Alito, J.); Wash. State Grange v. Wash. State Republican Party, 552 U.S. 442, 450 (2008) (Thomas, J.); Legal Servs. Corp. v. Velazquez, 531 U.S. 533, 545 (2001) (Kennedy, J.); Vt. Agency of Natural Res. v. United States *ex rel*. Stevens, 529 U.S. 765, 787 (2000) (Scalia, J.); Jones v. United States, 529 U.S. (continued...)

Standing Doctrine and the *Roberts* Court: *Hollingsworth & Amnesty Int'l*

The recent jurisprudence of the Roberts Court has, at times, relied on a rule cited by Justice Brandeis's *Ashwander* concurrence that the "Court will not pass upon the validity of a statute" when the plaintiff has "failed to show that he is injured by its operation,"[101] a rule that has taken on a constitutional dimension in the years since *Ashwander*. Specifically, whenever an individual "invo[kes] ... [a] federal court['s] jurisdiction" and formally asks a federal court to exercise its "remedial powers on his [or her] behalf,"[102] the Supreme Court has interpreted the case-or-controversy requirement of Article III of the Constitution such that the "party seeking judicial resolution of a dispute [must] 'show that he personally has suffered some actual or threatened injury as a result of the putatively illegal conduct'" of the other party.[103] The injury must be both "concrete and particularized" and "actual or imminent, not conjectural or hypothetical."[104] In addition to suffering an injury, the "irreducible constitutional minimum" of "standing" also requires that there be a "causal connection" between the injury and the conduct that is complained of, such that the injury is "fairly traceable" to the challenged action.[105] Finally, constitutional standing requires that it be likely that the injury will be redressed by a favorable decision.[106]

In contrast to the Article III concept of standing, the *Ashwander* concurrence and its progeny frames the issue of standing (and more generally, the doctrine of constitutional avoidance) as a prudential matter that can be invoked by the discretion of a federal court.[107] Nonetheless, the rationale for constitutional standing stems from many of the values implicit in the works of Professors Bickel and Sunstein. Specifically, the constitutional standing doctrine stems from the recognition that a federal court, in exercising judicial power, has the ability to "profoundly affect the lives, liberty, and property of those to whom it extends,"[108] and, accordingly, the power to seek relief from a federal court must be placed in the hands of those who have a "direct stake" in the outcome of the case and not merely in the "hands of 'concerned bystanders.'"[109] In turn, having parties with a "personal stake" in the outcome of the case "assure[s] ... concrete

---

(...continued)

848, 857 (2000) (Ginsburg, J.). Two of the Justices have cited Alexander Bickel as embodying their views on constitutional law. *See* John G. Roberts, Jr., *Chief Justice Interview on the Constitution,* C-SPAN, (June 25, 2011), http://www.c-span.org/video/?193515-1/chief-justice-interview-constitution (answering a question about a book that was "particularly important to [him] when it comes to the Constitution" with the response "books by people like Alexander Bickel.... ") ("Adam J. White, *The Burkean Justice,* THE WEEKLY STANDARD, (July 18, 2011), *available at* http://www.weeklystandard.com/articles/burkean-justice_576470 html?page=3 (quoting a 1985 letter written by Samuel Alito, citing the "writings of Alexander Bickel advocating judicial restraint" as inspiration to go to Yale Law School).

[101] 297 U.S. at 347 (Brandeis, J., concurring).

[102] *See* Simon v. Eastern Kentucky Welfare Rights Org., 426 U.S. 26, 38 (1976) (quoting Warth v. Seldin, 422 U.S. 490, 498-99 (1975)).

[103] *See* Diamond v. Charles, 476 U.S. 54, 62 (1986).

[104] *See* Lujan v. Defenders of Wildlife, 504 U.S. 555, 560 (1992).

[105] *Id.*

[106] *Id.*

[107] 297 U.S. at 347 (Brandeis, J., concurring); *but see* Lexmark Int'l, Inc. v. Static Control Components, Inc., 134 S. Ct. 1377, 1388 (2014) ("Just as a court cannot apply its independent policy judgment to recognize a cause of action that Congress has denied, it cannot limit a cause of action that Congress has created merely because 'prudence' dictates.").

[108] Valley Forge Christian College v. Americans United for Separation of Church and State, Inc., 454 U.S. 464, 473 (1982).

[109] *Diamond,* 476 U.S. at 62.

adverseness which sharpens the presentation of issues upon which the court so largely depends for illumination," allowing the court to be properly informed of the competing values before it.[110] Perhaps more importantly, standing has its roots in the countermajoritarian difficulty, as the doctrine is based, in part, on limiting the Court's interference with the decisions made by the political branches.[111] Echoing Professor Bickel's advocacy for the "passive virtues," Justice O'Connor noted in *Allen v. Wright* that the standing doctrine "makes possible the gradual clarification of the law through judicial application" and ensures that federal courts "exercise power only 'in the last resort, and as a necessity.'"[112]

The October 2012 term witnessed the Roberts Court avoiding ruling on two of the most controversial legal issues currently being debated in the United States through the use of the standing doctrine. First, in *Clapper v. Amnesty International,* the Court avoided opining on the constitutionality of certain foreign surveillance practices conducted by the executive branch through the use of the standing doctrine.[113] Specifically, *Amnesty International* presented a constitutional challenge to Section 702 of the Foreign Intelligence Surveillance Act of 1978 (FISA), a 2008 amendment to FISA that generally provides the federal government with the authority to engage in eavesdropping to gather intelligence information from foreign nations and non-state actors.[114] The Court, in a 5-4 ruling written by Justice Alito, held that the plaintiffs—a group of lawyers and human rights activists who claimed that Section 702 deterred their ability to speak with overseas clients who may be subject to foreign surveillance—lacked standing to bring the lawsuit, as the plaintiffs had failed to demonstrate that their alleged injuries arising from the 2008 law would be "certainly impending," as opposed to being merely probable.[115] In so doing, the Court noted that its ruling was based in part out of concern for the countermajoritarian difficulty. Specifically, Justice Alito noted that the ruling, at its base, was founded on "separation-of-powers principles" that "serve[] to prevent the judicial process from being used to usurp the powers of the political branches," a purpose that is particularly important with respect to the politically sensitive "fields of intelligence gathering and foreign affairs."[116]

Second, in *Hollingsworth v. Perry,* the last opinion issued by the Roberts Court during the October 2012 term, the Court again declined to rule on the merits of a controversial constitutional law question—the constitutionality of a state ban on same-sex marriage—and instead opted to resolve the case on standing grounds.[117] Specifically, in *Hollingsworth,* the Court considered an Equal Protection and Due Process challenge to Proposition 8, a law that amended the California Constitution to provide that only marriage between a man and a woman is valid or recognized in

---

[110] *See* Baker v. Carr, 369 U.S. 186, 204 (1962); *see also Valley Forge Christian College,* 454 U.S. at 473 ("[Standing] tends to assure that the legal questions presented to the court will be resolved, not in the rarified atmosphere of a debating society, but in a concrete factual context conducive to a realistic appreciation of the consequences of judicial action.").

[111] *Warth,* 422 U.S. at 498-99 (noting that Article III standing is "founded in concern about the proper—and properly limited—role of the courts in a democratic society.").

[112] 468 U.S. 737, 752 (1984) (internal citations omitted).

[113] *See* 568 U.S. __, 133 S.Ct. 1138 (2013).

[114] *See* 50 U.S.C. § 1881a.

[115] *See Amnesty Int'l,* 133 S.Ct. at 1150; *compare* Susan B. Anthony List v. Driehaus, 134 S. Ct. 2334, 2341 (2014) ("An allegation of future injury may suffice if the threatened injury is certainly impending, *or* there is a substantial risk that the harm will occur.") (internal citations and quotations omitted) (emphasis added).

[116] 133 S.Ct. at 1147. For a broader discussion of the *Amnesty International* decision, *see* CRS Report R43107, *Foreign Surveillance and the Future of Standing to Sue Post-Clapper* , by Andrew Nolan.

[117] 133 S. Ct. 2652 (2013).

California.[118] Because the state officials had declined to appeal an adverse district court ruling, the official "proponents"[119] of the proposition defended the law on appeal, prompting the question of whether the proponents had standing to appeal the district court's decision.[120] The Court, in 5-4 ruling written by the Chief Justice, held that the appellants lacked standing to defend Proposition 8 on appeal, as they lacked a "direct stake" in the outcome of their appeal and "their only interest in having the District Court order reversed was to vindicate the constitutional validity of a generally applicable California law."[121] In rejecting what the Court viewed as a "generalized grievance," the Court emphasized the standing doctrine's role in avoiding the potential perils of the countermajoritarian difficulty.[122] Specifically, the Court noted that by "[r]efusing to entertain generalized grievances," the Court "respects 'the proper—and properly limited—role of the courts in a democratic society.'"[123]

In the wake of both *Amnesty International* and *Hollingsworth*, new litigants with far stronger standing defenses have brought nearly identical constitutional claims to those heard in both 2013 rulings. For example, following the Court's ruling in *Amnesty International*, litigants who unquestionably have suffered an injury because of Section 702 of FISA—criminal defendants who are being prosecuted because of evidence obtained under the authority provided by the 2008 law—have begun to challenge Section 702 in district courts throughout the country, meaning the Court may, in the near future, revisit the underlying Fourth Amendment question posed by the *Amnesty International* litigants.[124] Similarly, after *Hollingsworth,* a host of challenges to various prohibitions on same-sex marriage have been defended by state officials who unquestionably have the authority under state law, and therefore have suffered the requisite injury, to defend a same-sex marriage ban.[125] In this sense, *Amnesty International* and *Hollingsworth* both illustrate the Roberts Court's use of one of the "passive virtues"—the standing doctrine—to "stay its hand" on major constitutional law questions, allowing those questions to percolate in the lower courts and in the political branches until the Court can more confidently resolve the underlying issues in the case.[126]

---

[118] *Id.* at 2659.

[119] Under Cal. Elec. Code Ann. §342, "[p]roponents of an initiative or referendum measure' means ... the elector or electors who submit the text of a proposed initiative or referendum to the Attorney General ... ; or ... the person or persons who publish a notice or intention to circulate petitions, or, where publication is not required, who file petitions with the elections official or legislative body."

[120] *Hollingsworth,* 133 S. Ct. at 2661. The Court also rejected the proposition that the referendum proponents were formally authorized to litigate on behalf of the State of California. *Id.* at 2664. For an extended discussion about *Hollingsworth* and the agency theory of standing, *see* CRS Report R43260, *Reform of the Foreign Intelligence Surveillance Courts: Introducing a Public Advocate*, by Andrew Nolan, Richard M. Thompson II, and Vivian S. Chu, at pp. 36-38.

[121] *Id.* at 2662.

[122] *Id.*

[123] *Id.* at 2667 (internal citations omitted).

[124] *See* CRS Report R43459, *Overview of Constitutional Challenges to NSA Collection Activities and Recent Developments*, by Edward C. Liu, Andrew Nolan, and Richard M. Thompson II, at pp. 14-15.

[125] *See* CRS Report R43481, *Same-Sex Marriage: A Legal Background After United States v. Windsor*, by Alison M. Smith, at pp. 5-6.

[126] *See generally* Richard M. Re, *Relative Standing,* 102 Geo. L.J. 1191, 1244-1249 (2014) (discussing the relationship between *Amnesty International* and *Hollingsworth*).

Last Resort Rule, the Avoidance Canon, and *Bond*

The standing doctrine is not the only rule invoked in Justice Brandeis's *Ashwander* concurrence that the Roberts Court has relied on in recent years. In fact, in one of the most anticipated cases[127] of the October 2013 term—*Bond v. United States*[128]—the Court invoked two of the *Ashwander* rules in resolving the case: the "last resort rule" and the "avoidance canon." The last resort rule states that a court should "not pass upon a constitutional question ... if there is also present some other ground upon which the case may be disposed of."[129] The rule tends to be invoked when a party that claims "relief on federal constitutional grounds also asserts a right to relief under a federal statute or regulations or on state law grounds."[130] The avoidance canon is a rule of statutory construction that states that "[w]hen the validity of an act ... is drawn in question, and even if a serious doubt of constitutionality is raised, ... [the Court] will first ascertain whether a construction of the statute is fairly possible by which the question may be avoided."[131] The avoidance canon has been described as the "most important and controversial" of the avoidance rules.[132]

Bond concerned the ability of the federal government to prosecute an embittered spouse, Carol Anne Bond, who had attempted to poison her husband's lover by coating her car door handles and mailbox with a mixture of toxic chemicals purchased on Amazon.com.[133] Federal prosecutors charged Ms. Bond with violating 18 U.S.C. Section 229, the Chemical Weapons Convention Implementation Act (CWCIA), which prohibits a person from "knowingly" "us[ing]" a "chemical weapon."[134] In turn, the CWCIA defines the term "chemical weapon" in a broad manner to include using a "toxic chemical"—that is, "*any* chemical through its chemical action on life processes can cause death, temporary incapacitation, or permanent harm to humans or animals."[135] On its face, the statute arguably applied to the conduct of Carol Bond when she attempted to expose her romantic rival to an arsenic-based compound and potassium dichromate, a combination that was, according to the Court, "toxic to humans" and "potentially lethal" in high doses.[136] In her defense, Ms. Bond challenged whether the application of the CWCIA to a purely local crime was constitutionally valid, as, in her view, the law "exceeded Congress's enumerated powers and invaded powers reserved to the States by the Tenth Amendment."[137] The government defended Bond's challenge to the statute, arguing that the CWCIA was constitutionally enacted according to the President's constitutional treaty making power, coupled with the power of

---

[127] *See, e.g.*, Marty Lederman, *Obeservations on the Oral Arguments in* Bond, JUST SECURITY,(Nov. 6, 2013), http://justsecurity.org/2931/observations-oral-argument-bond/ (noting that *Bond* "could turn out to be a landmark case.... ").

[128] 564 U.S. __, 134 S.Ct. 2077, 2083 (2014).

[129] *Ashwander*, 297 U.S. at 347 (Brandeis, J., concurring).

[130] *See* Fallon, *supra* note 23, at 87.

[131] *Ashwander*, 297 U.S. at 348 (Brandeis, J., concurring). For an extended discussion of the avoidance canon, *see* CRS Report 97-589, *Statutory Interpretation: General Principles and Recent Trends*, by Larry M. Eig, at pp. 23-24.

[132] *See* Fallon, *supra* note 23, at 88.

[133] *See Bond,* 134 S. Ct. at 2085.

[134] *Id.* The CWCIA does have several exceptions from its general prohibition, including the use of a toxic chemical for "peaceful purposes," such as industrial, agricultural, research, medical, or pharmaceutical activities. *See* 18 U.S.C. § 229F(7)(A). None of the exclusions were found applicable in *Bond. See Bond,* 134 S. Ct. at 2086.

[135] 18 U.S.C. § 229F(8)(A) (emphasis added).

[136] *See Bond,* 134 S. Ct. at 2085.

[137] *Id.*

Congress to enact legislation that is "necessary and proper" to carry into execution the treaty power.[138] In short, the *Bond* case presented the Court with "significant" and long-debated constitutional questions respecting the "powers of federalism" and the scope of the treaty power.[139]

Nonetheless, invoking the *Ashwander* doctrine, Chief Justice Roberts, writing for a six-person majority, declined to reach the weighty constitutional issues posed by Ms. Bond's prosecution. The *Bond* opinion avoided the constitutional question regarding the scope of the treaty power by first noting that Ms. Bond raised a non-constitutional argument in her defense—that Section 229 did "not cover her conduct."[140] Citing to Justice Brandeis's concurrence, Chief Justice Roberts invoked the last resort rule, stating that the "Court will not decide a constitutional question if there is some other ground upon which to dispose of the case."[141] As a result, the Court turned to the statutory question, and, relying on the avoidance canon, the Court held that the CWCIA simply did not reach Ms. Bond's activities.[142] For the Court, because under the Constitution Congress "possesses only limited powers" and typically does not have the power to criminalize "an act committed wholly within a State," the CWCIA should "be read consistent with the principles of federalism inherent in our constitutional structure."[143] While the term "chemical weapon" as used in the CWCIA has a potentially broad import, Chief Justice Roberts concluded that without a "clear indication" from Congress that Section 229 was to be read so expansively to reach purely local matters, the term "chemical weapon" in the act must be read narrowly and in light of the specific purposes of the CWC to prevent chemical warfare.[144] As such, just as the Court refused to reach questions regarding the constitutional propriety of U.S. foreign surveillance efforts and same-sex marriage bans in the October 2012 term, so too *Bond* arguably demonstrated a continued hesitancy by the Roberts Court to resolve divisive political issues through the process of judicial review.

Judicial Minimalism and the *Roberts* Court

Perhaps of all of the *Ashwander* rules, the one relied on by the Roberts Court most frequently is the rule that forms the basis of Professor Sunstein's judicial minimalism: the Court should not "formulate a rule of constitutional law broader than is required by the precise facts to which it is applied."[145] Notwithstanding rulings like *Citizens United* and *NFIB*,[146] constitutional law scholars

---

[138] *Id.*

[139] *See* Scott Bomboy, *A Supreme Court love triangle case that could make history*, CONSTITUTION DAILY (May 12, 2014), http://blog.constitutioncenter.org/2014/05/the-supreme-courts-love-triangle-case-could-make-history/. For an extended discussion of *Bond* and the constitutional issues posed by the case, *see* CRS Report R42968, *Bond v. United States: Validity and Construction of the Federal Chemical Weapons Statute*, by Charles Doyle.

[140] *See Bond,* 134 S. Ct. at 2087.

[141] *Id.* (internal citations omitted).

[142] *Id.* at 2090.

[143] *Id.* at 2088.

[144] *Id.* at 2093.

[145] *Ashwander*, 297 U.S. at 347 (Brandeis, J., concurring).

[146] *See* Laurence H. Tribe, *What Should Congress Do About* Citizens United?, (Jan. 24, 2010), http://www.scotusblog.com/2010/01/what-should-congress-do-about-citizens-united/ ("There is no doubt that Citizens United v. Federal Election Commission marks a major upheaval in First Amendment law and signals the end of whatever legitimate claim could otherwise have been made by the Roberts Court to an incremental and minimalist approach to constitutional adjudication, to a modest view of the judicial role vis-a -vis the political branches, or to a genuine concern with adherence to precedent.").

have frequently described the Roberts Court as being minimalist in nature.[147] Indeed, recent scholarship comparing aggregate voting patterns of the Roberts and the Rehnquist Courts has concluded that the Roberts Court is "considerably more minimalist" and "there has been a decided shift in favor of minimalist behavior since Roberts became Chief."[148] And while a lively debate exists over whether the Roberts Court's use of minimalism is sufficiently minimalist or should be equated with judicial modesty,[149] the last two terms of the Roberts Court have witnessed the Court embracing some form of minimalism in its constitutional law jurisprudence, with the Court issuing rulings that could have had the potential to be far broader in their implications and were largely limited to the facts of the case at hand.[150]

For example, in the final week of the October 2012 term, the Court issued three rulings that arguably exemplify the Roberts Court's embrace of more "narrow" and "shallow" rulings in constitutional law cases. For example, on June 24, 2013, the Court issued a 7-1 ruling in *Fisher v. University of Texas,* reversing a lower court decision upholding the University of Texas's affirmative action program.[151] However, in lieu of, as some suspected, issuing a broad ruling settling long-debated questions on the constitutionality of affirmative action in higher education,[152] the Court resolved the case on the more narrow ground that the lower court in *Fisher* had inappropriately deferred to University of Texas's judgment about the necessity of the affirmative action program in achieving diversity, a judgment that implicitly reaffirmed that diversity could serve as a compelling interest justifying affirmative action under the Equal Protection Clause of the Fourteenth Amendment.[153] In other words, *Fisher* was a ruling that was

---

[147] *See, e.g., See Artemus Ward & J. Mitchell Pickerill, Judicial Minimalism Is Alive and Well on the Roberts Court,* NAT'L L.J. (July 3, 2013), http://www.nationallawjournal.com/id=1202609561827 ("Instead, narrow, minimalist rulings are now the order of the day. In each case, Roberts voted for a narrow position and his view prevailed in three of the four decisions. In the case where it did not- Windsor-he drafted a dissent emphasizing that the Court's holding was limited."); Hans Bader, Free Enterprise Fund v. PCAOB: *Narrow Separation-of-Powers Ruling Illustrates That the Supreme Court Is Not "Pro-Business",* 2010 CATO SUP. CT. REV. 269, 269 ("Chief Justice John Roberts has often been depicted as an advocate of narrow rulings and a judicial philosophy of minimalism."); Randall T. Adams, Note, *Recent Development:* Northwest Austin Municipal Utility District Number One v. Holder, 45 HARV. C.R.-C.L. L. REV. 135, 135 (2010) (noting a series of decisions by the Roberts Court "that might be fairly characterized as 'minimalist'").

[148] *See* J. Mitchell Pickerill and Artemus Ward, *Measuring Judicial Minimalism on the Roberts Court,* (August 21, 2013). Available at SSRN: http://ssrn.com/abstract=2314135 or http://dx.doi.org/10.2139/ssrn.2314135 (concluding that the aggregate votes of the justices on the Roberts Court were minimalist 76.7% of the time, compared to 54.7% for the Rehnquist Court). This scholarship echoes earlier studies of the Roberts Court. *See* Robert Anderson IV, *Measuring Meta-Doctrine: An Empirical Assessment of Judicial Minimalism in the Supreme Court,* 32 HARV. J.L. & PUB. POL'Y 1045, 1089-1090 (2009) (noting that the preliminary data from the "Roberts Court suggests that minimalist need not worry about a major change in the minimalism of the Court" and that Roberts "may be among the more minimalist members of the Court.... ").

[149] *See, e.g.,* Richard L. Hasen, *The Chief Justice's Long Game,* N.Y TIMES (June 25, 2013), http://www nytimes.com/2013/06/26/opinion/the-chief-justices-long-game html?_r=0; Scott Lemieux, *The Maximalist Supreme Court,* The American Prospect, (April 13, 2011), http://prospect.org/article/maximalist-supreme-court.

[150] *Cf.* Sunstein, *supra* note 64, at 10-13.

[151] 570 U.S. __, 133 S. Ct. 2411.

[152] *See* Cass R. Sunstein, *Judicial Minimalism Triumphs in Affirmative Action Case,* BLOOMBERGVIEW (June 24, 2013), http://www.bloombergview.com/articles/2013-06-24/judicial-minimalism-triumphs-in-affirmative-action-case ("In Fisher, many people hoped—or feared—that a majority of the court would take the opportunity to insist on colorblindness."). For an extended discussion of the constitutional issues raised by *Fisher, see* CRS Report RL30410, *Affirmative Action and Diversity in Public Education: Legal Developments,* by Jody Feder.

[153] *Fisher,* 133 S. Ct. at 2420 ("The University must prove that the means chosen by the University to attain diversity are narrowly tailored to that goal. On this point, the University receives no deference.").

---

both confined to the facts of the case and narrow in its holding, epitomizing Sunstein's minimalism.[154]

Three days later, the Court, in *Shelby County v. Holder,* struck down Section 4(b) of the Voting Rights Act (VRA),[155] a portion of the act that contains the coverage formula that determines what jurisdictions' voting laws are subject to preclearance by the federal government before a given law can go into effect.[156] While *Shelby County*'s holding has been criticized by some,[157] the decision did not go so far as some, such as Justice Thomas, would have wished.[158] Specifically, the Court declined to reach the question of whether Section 5 of the VRA, which establishes the preclearance formula, was constitutionally permissible.[159] Instead, the Court went so far as to invite Congress to reenact a more specific and updated version of the coverage formula.[160] As a result, an argument can be made that *Shelby County* can be viewed as a narrow opinion that does not wholly foreclose all democratic debate on the underlying constitutional issues, the hallmarks of a minimalist decision.[161]

A day later, the Court issued its ruling in *United States v. Windsor,* striking down Section 3 of DOMA, finding that the law's "traditional" definition for marriage amounted to a "deprivation of the equal liberty of persons that [is] protected by the Fifth Amendment."[162] While the ruling in *Windsor* certainly will have implications for future litigation on same-sex marriage bans,[163] the *Windsor* Court confined its ruling to the specific issues posed by the case—the constitutionality of Section 3 of DOMA denying federal benefits to *married* same-sex couples.[164] In other words, the Court in *Windsor* declined to opine more broadly on the constitutional legitimacy of a state prohibition on same-sex marriage, leaving that issue for another day.[165]

---

[154] *See* Sunstein, *supra* note 151.

[155] 570 U.S. __, 133 S. Ct. 2612 (2013).

[156] *See* 42 U.S.C. § 1973b(b).

[157] *See, e.g.,* Richard L. Hasen, *Shelby County and the Illusion of Minimalism,* 22 WM. & MARY BILL OF RTS. J. 713 (2014) ("Despite the projected judicial modesty, the Shelby County Court was doing much more than calling balls and strikes and applying settled precedent to uncontested facts. Shelby County is an audacious opinion which ignores history, declines to engage the dissent's powerful argument that the VRA's bailout provisions solve any constitutional problem, and rejects the Roberts Court's stated commitment to judicial minimalism in its treatment of facial challenges and severability.").

[158] *See* 133 S. Ct. at 2631 (Thomas, J., concurring).

[159] *Id.* at 2631 ("We issue no holding on §5 itself, only on the coverage formula. Congress may draft another formula based on current conditions.").

[160] *Id.*

[161] *Cf.* Sunstein, *supra* note 64, at 4; *but see* Hasen, *supra* note 156, at 713. For more on *Shelby County, see* CRS Report R42482, *Congressional Redistricting and the Voting Rights Act: A Legal Overview*, by L. Paige Whitaker, at pp. 9-11.

[162] 570 U.S. __, 133 S. Ct. 2675, 2695 (2013).

[163] *See* Smith, *supra* note 125, at pp. 5-6.

[164] *See* 133 S.Ct. at 2696 ("By seeking to displace this protection and treating those persons as living in marriages less respected than others, the federal statute is in violation of the Fifth Amendment. This opinion and its holding are confined to those lawful marriages.").

[165] *See id.* at 2696 (Roberts, C.J., dissenting) ("I think it more important to point out that its analysis leads no further. The Court does not have before it, and the logic of its opinion does not decide, the distinct question whether the States, in the exercise of their "historic and essential authority to define the marital relation,".... may continue to utilize the traditional definition of marriage.").

The October 2013 term of the Roberts Court similarly showed a tendency toward minimalism in even the most controversial of the Court's rulings. For example, in *Schuette v. Coalition to Defend Affirmative Action,* the Court upheld the constitutionality of the state of Michigan's referendum prohibiting the use of race-based preferences as part of the admissions process for state universities.[166] In so doing, in contrast to the concurring opinion of Justice Scalia,[167] the controlling plurality of the Court refused to overturn nearly 50-year-old precedent holding that the Fourteenth Amendment prohibited restructuring the political process in such a way that diminished the participatory rights of minorities.[168] Instead, as noted in the concurring opinion of Justice Breyer, *Schuette* was distinguished from the so-called "political process doctrine" cases on the grounds that the Michigan referendum did not diminish the political participation of minority voters because the referendum merely moved decision-making authority from unelected actors (school administrators) and "placed it in the hands of the voters."[169] Similarly, Justice Kennedy's plurality opinion confined the ruling to the unique facts presented by the Michigan referendum at issue in *Schuette* and refused to question the continued viability of the political process doctrine.[170]

Likewise in a public employee free speech case, *Lane v. Franks,*[171] Justice Sotomayor's unanimous opinion declined to question the validity of the much-debated[172] *Garcetti v. Ceballos* decision, a 2006 case that held that "when public employees make statements pursuant to their official duties, the employees are not speaking as citizens for First Amendment purposes, and the Constitution does not insulate their communications from employer discipline."[173] Instead, in *Lane*, the Supreme Court narrowly tailored its opinion to the facts of the case before the Court, holding that the First Amendment "protects a public employee who provides truthful sworn testimony, compelled by subpoena, outside the scope of his ordinary job responsibilities."[174] In this sense, the ruling in *Lane* can be viewed as a narrow opinion tied to the particular facts of the case with limited import for the central holding of *Garcetti*.[175]

On the final day of the October 2013 term, the Court issued another arguably minimalist opinion in *Harris v. Quinn*. In *Harris,* Justice Alito, in a 5-4 ruling, struck down on First Amendment

---

[166] *See* 134 S. Ct. 1623.

[167] *Id.* at 1639 (Scalia, J., concurring).

[168] *Id.* at 1637-38; *see also id.* at 1650 (Breyer, J., concurring) ("*Hunter* and *Seattle* involved efforts to manipulate the political process in a way not here at issue.").

[169] *Id.* at 1650 (Breyer, J., concurring).

[170] *Id.* at 1638 (distinguishing *Hunter* and *Seattle* on the grounds that those cases "were ones in which the political restriction in question was designed to be used, or was likely to be used, to encourage infliction of injury by reason of race."). For more on the constitutional issues raised by the *Schuette* decision, *see* CRS Report R43205, *Banning the Use of Racial Preferences in Higher Education: A Legal Analysis of Schuette v. Coalition to Defend Affirmative Action*, by Jody Feder.

[171] 573 U.S. ___, 134 S. Ct. 2369.

[172] *See, e.g.,* Julie A. Wenell, Garcetti v. Ceballos: *Stifling the First Amendment in the Public Workplace,* 16 WM. & MARY BILL OF RTS. J. 623 (2007); Kermit Roosevelt III, *Not as Bad as You Think: Why* Garcetti v. Ceballos *Makes Sense,* 14 U. PA. J. CONST. L. 631 (2012).

[173] 547 U.S. 410, 421 (2006).

[174] 134 S. Ct. at 2378.

[175] *See id.* at 2383-84 (Thomas, J., concurring) ("This case presents a discrete question ... We accordingly have no occasion to address the quite different question whether a public employee speaks 'as a citizen' when he testifies in the course of his ordinary job responsibilities."). For a discussion of specific legal issues at play in *Lane, see* CRS Report WSLG983, *Reading the Fine Print: Why Footnotes Matter in Lane v. Franks*, by Andrew Nolan and Valerie Bieberich.

grounds an Illinois law requiring personal health assistants paid under the state-run Medicaid program to pay the "fair share" of the due to a public employee union.[176] In so doing, the Court severely criticized *Abood v. Detroit Board of Education,*[177] the central precedent that generally allows state employees who choose not to join a public-sector union to be compelled to pay an agency fee to support union work related to the collective-bargaining process.[178] Nonetheless, the Court did not go so far as to formally overrule *Abood,*[179] keeping its decision confined to the "new situation ... before" the Court—that is, the question of whether "quasi-public employees" like the personal assistants in *Harris* could be compelled to pay public union dues.[180] In short, *Harris* mirrors themes from *Lane* and *Schuette,* by eschewing a broad constitutional ruling that overrules past precedent in favor of a more narrow and confined opinion.

Criticisms of Constitutional Avoidance

Notwithstanding the near omnipresence of the constitutional avoidance doctrine at the Roberts Court, the doctrine and the work of Professors Bickel and Sunstein are not without their critics, both inside and outside of the Court. In fact, the doctrine has been attacked both with respect to its underlying assumptions and to how the doctrine has been deployed. In addition, the different strands of the constitutional avoidance doctrine, such as the rule counseling judicial minimalism and the constitutional avoidance canon, have been critically assessed by both legal scholars and jurists.

Criticisms Related to the Underlying Rationale of Constitutional Avoidance

The idea that courts should actively avoid resolving constitutional disputes arguably stands in contrast to the role envisioned for the federal courts by Alexander Hamilton in the Federalist Papers and echoed by Chief Justice John Marshall in *Marbury.* In noting that interpreting the law is the "proper and peculiar province of the courts," Hamilton in *Federalist #78* argued that the federal courts have the "superior obligation" to prefer the "fundamental law" of the Constitution to any law passed by a legislature.[181] Echoing Hamilton's themes nearly 200 years later, Professor Herbert Wechsler wrote in what was once the second most cited law review article[182] that courts have "both the title and duty when a case is properly before them to review the actions of the other branches in light of constitutional provisions.... "[183] For Wechsler and his disciples, courts "cannot escape the duty of deciding whether actions of the other branches of government are

---

[176] 573 U.S. __, 134 S. Ct. 2618, 2625 (2014).

[177] 431 U.S. 209 (1977).

[178] 134 S. Ct. at 2627-34 (noting that the "*Abood* Court's analysis is questionable on several grounds.").

[179] *Id.* at 2638 n.19 ("It is therefore unnecessary for us to reach petitioners' argument that Abood should be overruled, and the dissent's extended discussion of stare decisis is beside the point.").

[180] *Id.* at 2638. For a brief discussion of the constitutional law issues raised by *Harris, see* CRS Report WSLG1004, *Court Rejects Agency Fees for "Quasi-Public" Employees,* by Jon O. Shimabukuro.

[181] *See* THE FEDERALIST, No. 78, at 435 (Alexander Hamilton) (Clinton Rossiter ed., 1999).

[182] Fred R. Shapiro, *The Most-Cited Law Review Articles,* 73 CALIF. L. REV. 1540, 1549 (1985).

[183] Herbert Wechsler, *Toward Neutral Principles of Constitutional Law,* 73 HARV. L. REV. 1, 19 (1959).

consistent with the Constitution," raising the question of whether the avoidance doctrine is a means by which a court can evade its most basic constitutional duties.[184]

The criticism that constitutional avoidance is diametrically opposed to the Court's constitutional duties finds favor from both judicial conservatives and liberals. With respect to the former, jurists like Justice Antonin Scalia, in contrast to Professor Bickel's suggestion that the Supreme Court should protect fundamental principles of our society—including "the evolving morality of our tradition"—embrace a view that the Court should protect "permanent," as opposed to "evolving," values that are embodied in an understanding of the original intent of the Framers.[185] As a consequence, when a constitutional question is properly presented to the Court and the original understanding of the Constitution dictates a particular result, jurists like Justice Scalia reject the idea that the Court should "stay" its hand in answering the question presented.[186] In this vein, Justice Scalia's concurrence in *Bond* voiced his disagreement with the Chief Justice's majority opinion that avoided the constitutional question regarding the treaty power posed by the case, arguing that the Court "shirk[ed] its job" in failing to reach the constitution issue.[187]

Other jurists who envision the Supreme Court's constitutional role to be centered on improving the democratic character of the political process may voice slightly different disagreements with the avoidance doctrine. Such a judicial philosophy is perhaps best represented by the "most famous footnote in all of constitutional law,"[188] footnote four of *United States v. Carolene Products.*[189] Footnote four discusses when the "presumption of constitutionality" should not stand and democratically enacted law should be subject to more "exacting judicial scrutiny."[190] Specifically, laws that violate rights that are preconditions for a functioning democracy and laws that uniquely prejudice groups that may be excluded from the democratic process "may call for" a "more searching judicial inquiry."[191] For jurists who embrace footnote four's view of judicial review, the constitutional avoidance doctrine can be seen as being contrary to the judiciary's central constitutional role, as avoiding a constitutional ruling or issuing a "minimalist" constitutional ruling in a case respecting the functioning of the democracy obviates the role of the judiciary in protecting core civil rights. As such, Justice Sotomayor, in her dissenting opinion in *Schuette*, decried the plurality's narrow reading of the political process doctrine, as she "firmly believe[s]" that the role of judges includes broadly "policing the process of self-government and stepping in when necessary to secure the constitutional guarantee of equal protection."[192]

---

[184] *Id.* at 10.

[185] *See* Antonin Scalia, *Originalism: The Lesser Evil*, 57 U CIN. L. REV. 849, 862-64 (1989).

[186] *Id.* at 854 (criticizing nonoriginalism as incompatible with judicial review); *see also* Adrian Vermeule, LAW AND THE LIMITS OF REASON 5 (2009) (criticizing common law constitutionalism's tendency to raise judicially established precedent above both constitutional and statutory text and original meanings).

[187] 134 S. Ct. at 2094 (Scalia, J., concurring).

[188] *See* Sunstein, *supra* note 64, at 7.

[189] 304 U.S. 144, 153 n.4 (1938).

[190] *Id.*

[191] *Id.*

[192] 134 S. Ct. at 1654 (Sotomayor, J., dissenting).

Criticisms Related to How the Constitutional Avoidance Doctrine Is Used By Judges

Beyond the critiques related to the theoretical bases for the avoidance doctrine, the *Ashwander* doctrine has also been criticized because of the dangers in how the doctrine can be deployed by judges. Perhaps the most pointed criticism of Professor Bickel's work came from Professor Gerald Gunther in an article published two years after the release of the *Least Dangerous Branch*.[193] For Gunther, Bickel's "passive virtues" "are 'passive in name and appearance only," as Bickel's theories encourage a "free-wheeling interventionism" that allows judges to manipulate the various rules counseling restraint in an effort toward a particular result.[194] The concern that the "passive virtues" can be manipulated to produce desired judicial results has certainly been voiced in the context of discussions regarding the Court's jurisprudence on standing.[195] And this criticism is echoed in both (1) Justice Breyer's dissent in *Amnesty International*, where he contends that the majority opinion's view on standing is in contrast to what "commonsense inference and ordinary knowledge of human nature" dictates;[196] and (2) Justice Kennedy's dissent in *Hollingsworth*, where he accuses the majority opinion of "misconstruing the principles of justiciability to avoid the subject" of ruling on the constitutionality of a same-sex marriage ban.[197]

Beyond the issue of whether the "passive virtues" can be manipulated by judges, another central concern with respect to constitutional avoidance is the doctrine's lack of clarity with respect to when a constitutional question should be affirmatively answered. Professor Bickel argued that a genuinely principled Court "will enforce as law only the most widely shared values,"[198] but it may be impossible for the Supreme Court to determine what truly are "widely shared values" and when the judiciary has truly engaged in principled judicial review protecting such values.[199] As a result, constitutional avoidance can at times lead to inconsistent results by the judiciary. For example, one may question why on the same day the Court in *Hollingsworth* refused to rule on the merits of Proposition 8, the Court did reach the merits of the constitutionality of Section 3 of DOMA, despite perhaps even stronger reasons counseling the Court to "stay its hand" in the *Windsor* case. Specifically, the fact that both the plaintiff and defendant in *Windsor* agreed on the

---

[193] Gerald Gunther, *The Subtle Vices of the "Passive Virtues" - A Comment on Principle and Expediency in Judicial Review*, 64 COLUM. L. REV. 1 (1964).

[194] *Id.* at 25.

[195] *See, e.g.*, Richard J. Pierce, Jr., *Is Standing Law or Politics?*, 77 N.C. L. REV. 1741 (1999) ("Five Supreme Court decisions issued between 1991 and 1998 illustrate the accuracy of the political scientist's description of the law of standing ... Liberals voted to grant access to the courts to environmentalists, employees, and prisoners, but not to banks. Conservatives voted to grant access to banks, but not to environmentalists, employees, or prisoners. Of course, in each case, all the Justices claimed to reach their politically preferred result through objective application of legal doctrines. The applicable doctrines are so malleable, however, that it is impossible to avoid the inference that the Justices manipulated the doctrines to rationalize their politically preferred results.").

[196] *See* 133 S. Ct. at 1155 (Breyer, J., dissenting). Indeed, arguably the Court walked back from its decision on the standing question in *Amnesty International* one year later in *Susan B. Anthony List v. Driehaus*, where the Court held that a "substantial risk that [a] harm will occur" suffices to establish the needed injury for standing. *See* 134 S. Ct. at 2341; *see also* CRS Report WSLG999, Imminent Threats to Election Speech: Standing and Susan B. Anthony List, by Valerie Bieberich and Andrew Nolan (conparing Susan B. Anthony List and Amnesty International).

[197] *See* 133 S. Ct. at 2674 (Kennedy, J., dissenting).

[198] Bickel, *supra* note 18, at 239.

[199] *See* J. Skelly Wright, *Professor Bickel, the Scholarly Tradition, and the Supreme Court*, 84 HARV. L. REV. 769, 778 (1971) ("If past Courts have also systematically failed to meet the requirements of principled decision making, does this not suggest that the requirements themselves ... are fatally unrealistic?").

---

outcome of the case arguably made the case one of the rare instances of "friendly, non-adversary, proceeding" reaching the High Court.[200] The net result of *Windsor* and *Hollingsworth* was that the Court on the same day held that the official proponents of Proposition 8 did not have the requisite interest in the litigation to ensure that there was an adverse lawsuit before the Court, but that the Department of Justice's wholehearted agreement with the plaintiff in *Windsor* regarding the merits of her lawsuit did not destroy the adversity necessary for the Court to hear the case, a seemingly bizarre result that can potentially be attributed to the often unpredictable applications of the various *Ashwander* rules.

In addition to the arguably bizarre outcomes of the "gay marriage" cases, inconsistency has been—at times—the hallmark of the Court's treatment of another one of the *Ashwander* rules, the last resort rule, as the Court has at times created doctrines that necessitate or encourage making non-outcome-determinative rulings on constitutional questions as an initial matter in a case. For example, under the "harmless error" doctrine, a court will generally first determine whether a violation of the Constitution during the course of a criminal conviction occurred and only then will proceed to determine whether the error was harmless.[201] Moreover, pursuant to the "good faith" exception to the Fourth Amendment's exclusionary rule, a court, having found that a police officer's search was obtained in violation of the Constitution, will then allow the introduction of evidence if the officer's mistake was the result of negligence.[202] Perhaps the most common exception to the last resort rule occurs in the context of the qualified immunity doctrine, where the Court's precedent dictates that it is "often appropriate" for a court to first look at whether a government officer has violated the Constitution and then proceed to determine whether the violated right was "clearly established" at the time of the alleged violation to determine liability.[203]

Specific Criticisms of the *Ashwander* Rules

Beyond the various criticisms of the general concept of constitutional avoidance, many have voiced disagreements with specific *Ashwander* rules, including the rules promoting judicial minimalism and avoiding interpreting a law in a way that raises a constitutional issue.

Criticism of Judicial Minimalism

Justice Brandeis's rule requiring constitutional rulings to be on the narrowest possible grounds and Professor Sunstein's work on judicial minimalism have generated a robust debate amongst academics, which, much like the criticisms of the avoidance doctrine as a whole, has centered on both the *logic* of minimalism and how minimalism can be *deployed* by judges. With respect to the logic of minimalism, critics of Professor Sunstein have questioned the value of the Court issuing narrow and shallow rulings. Professor Neil Devins, for example, has argued that minimalism is "flawed" because federal judges, having life tenure, are "less likely to be driven by political expediency" and, therefore, are more capable than any other institution in government to

---

[200] *See* 133 S. Ct. 2675, 2699 (2013) (Scalia, J., dissenting) ("As Justice Brandeis put it, we cannot 'pass upon the constitutionality of legislation in a friendly, non-adversary, proceeding'; absent a 'real, earnest and vital controversy between individuals,' we have neither any work to do nor any power to do it.") (citing *Ashwander*).

[201] Kotteakos v. United States, 328 U.S. 750, 765 (1946).

[202] Herring v. United States, 555 U.S. 135, 147 (2009).

[203] Pearson v. Callahan, 555 U.S. 223, 236 (2009).

articulate broad principles of law to guide the other branches of government and society as a whole.[204] In contrast, according to Professor Devins, minimalist decisions are often "ambiguous" and "fact-specific," and, as a result, such decisions "lack[] moral force" and fail to influence government decision making.[205] Put another way, as then-Professor Neal Katyal noted in a 1998 law review defending the role of the federal judiciary as "advicegivers," while minimalism may have the advantage of "leaving ... courts out of many political disputes," the doctrine can be potentially "problematic because it often offers no guidance to the other branches about what is and is not permissible."[206]

The criticism that minimalist Supreme Court decisions fail to provide needed guidance and clarity has been voiced at times by members of the High Court. For example, in a much quoted letter, Justice Harlan Fiske Stone wrote to then-Professor Felix Frankfurter criticizing a narrow ruling by the Hughes Court, stating,

> I can hardly see the use of writing judicial opinions unless they are to embody methods of analysis and of exposition which will serve the profession as a guide to the decision of future cases. If they are not better than an excursion ticket, good for this day and trip only, they do not serve even as protective coloration for the writer of the opinion and would much better be left unsaid.[207]

Moreover, even when a Justice has agreed with the result in a particular case, that Justice may find fault with the narrow scope of the majority opinion. For example, in *NASA v. Nelson,* a 2011 decision rejecting that certain federal contract workers could voice constitutional objections to a "standard employment background investigation,"[208] Justice Scalia concurred in the judgment, scolding the majority for "assuming without deciding" that a constitutional right to informational privacy existed.[209] For Justice Scalia, by not resolving the scope of the underlying constitutional right, the majority opinion was a "vague" one that "provide[d] no guidance for the lower courts."[210] Justice Scalia closed his concurrence in *Nelson* by arguing that "Whatever the virtues of judicial minimalism, it cannot justify judicial incoherence" and by quoting from *Marbury's* famous command that the "judicial department" must "say what the law is."[211]

---

[204] Neal Devins, *The Courts: The Democracy-Forcing Constitution*, 97 MICH. L. REV. 1971, 1990 (1999)

[205] *Id.* 1990-91.

[206] Neal Kumar Katyal, *Judges as Advicegivers,* 50 STAN. L. REV. 1709, 1802 (1998). For a response to Katyal's work, *see* Abner Mikva, *Why Judges Should Not Be Advice-givers*, 50 STAN. L. REV. 1825 (1998). Some critics of minimalism would challenge Katyal's concession that minimalism allows the Supreme Court to avoid political disputes. For example, Professor Mark Tushnet, echoing Professor Gunther's criticisms of Bickel's work, has argued that minimalism is an "unsuitable doctrinal criterion" because if minimalism guides judicial decisionmaking, it necessitates the judges evaluating the "current state of public discussion" and determining "what decision will have the least impact on that discussion." *See* Mark Tushnet, *How To Deny a Constitutional Right: Reflections on the Assisted Suicide Cases*, 1 GREEN BAG 2D 55, 59-60 (1997); *see also* Mark Tushnet, *The Supreme Court 1998 Term Forward: The New Constitutional Order and the Chastening of Constitutional Aspiration,* 113 HARV. L. REV. 29, 95 (1999).

[207] *See* Justice Stone to Professor Frankfurter quoted in C. Miller, THE SUPREME COURT AND THE USES OF HISTORY 13 (1969).

[208] 562 U.S. 134, 131 S. Ct. 746 (2011).

[209] *Id.* at 767 (Scalia, J., concurring).

[210] *Id.*

[211] *Id.* at 767-69 (quoting *Marbury*). Justice Scalia's *Nelson* concurrence echoes themes from an earlier concurrence where he similarly objected to what he viewed to be an unnecessarily minimalist majority opinion. *See* Hein v. Freedom from Religion Found., Inc., 551 U.S. 587, 633 (2007) (Scalia, J., concurring) ("Minimalism is an admirable judicial trait, but not when it comes at the cost of meaningless and disingenuous distinctions that hold the sure promise (continued...)

Similarly, Justice Thomas has voiced concerns when an arguably minimalist majority opinion has provided insufficient guidance for the judiciary and the political branches. For example, in *Shelby County,* Justice Thomas concurred, arguing that the Court should not only have struck down the VRA's preclearance coverage *formula,* but that the Court should have taken the further step to invalidate Section 5 of the VRA that allows for federal preclearance of certain state election laws in the first place.[212] For Justice Thomas, the Court's more narrow ruling in *Shelby County* striking down the preclearance formula demonstrated the "the inevitable conclusion" that the concept of preclearance in and of itself was unconstitutional.[213] As a consequence, Justice Thomas, in his *Shelby County* concurrence, voiced disappointment that the Court did not rule more broadly and instead, in his view, "needlessly prolong[ed] the demise of [the preclearance] provision" contained in Section 5 of the VRA.[214]

Perhaps the most prevalent criticism of judicial minimalism focuses not so much on whether minimalism is a desirable goal for the Court, but instead centers on the consistency with which minimalism is applied and whether minimalism is used as a means toward certain political ends. Such criticism of minimalism has come from both ends of the political spectrum. Frequent Supreme Court practitioner Charles Cooper has condemned minimalism as a "litigation strategy designed to bring about judicial imposition of the liberal social agenda more gradually."[215] And Professor Sai Prakash has similarly argued that "[f]or many on the left minimalism and its respect for precedent is the flavor of the month" that will be discarded once a minimalist approach conflicts with the desired political outcome in a case.[216] At the same time, some legal progressives have been equally suspicious of judicial minimalism. Indeed, for many critics from the left, Chief Justice Roberts has "used the rhetoric of 'minimalism' and 'restraint' to" disguise what they see as deep substantive changes in constitutional law being pursued by the Court.[217] For example, in the wake of the *Shelby County* decision, Professor Richard Hasen wrote in an opinion piece in the *New York Times* arguing that Chief Justice Roberts's majority opinion "hides behind a cloak of judicial minimalism" an effort to "cripple[] Section 5 of the" VRA.[218] In this sense, in the view of Professor Hasen, the Chief Justice uses minimalism as a part of his "long game" to advance a conservative agenda on the Court.[219] Regardless of the truth of the criticisms of minimalism from

---

(...continued)

of engendering further meaningless and disingenuous distinctions in the future. The rule of law is ill served by forcing lawyers and judges to make arguments that deaden the soul of the law, which is logic and reason.").

[212] 133 S. Ct. at 2631 (Thomas, J., concurring).

[213] *Id.* at 2632.

[214] *Id.*

[215] *See* Charles J. Cooper, "Debate on Radicals in Robes," in INTRODUCTION TO ORIGINALISM: A QUARTER-CENTURY OF DEBATE 303 (Steven G. Calabresi ed. 2007) ("But minimalism is liberal judicial activism on the installment plan.").

[216] *See* Saikrishna Prakash, *Radicals in Tweed Jackets: Why Extreme Left Wing Law Professors are Wrong for America,* 106 COLUM. L. REV. 2207 (2006) ("When enough undesirable precedents accumulate, we will no doubt hear that minimalism is a theory that pays too much respect to the dead or the doddering and too little attention to the needs of the present.").

[217] *See* Josh Benson, *The Past Does Not Repeat Itself, but It Rhymes: The Second Coming of the Liberal Anti-Court Movement,* 33 LAW & SOC. INQUIRY 1071, 1075 & 1104-05 (2008).

[218] *See* Hasen, *supra* note 149.

[219] *Id.; see also* Adam Liptak, *Roberts Pulls Supreme Court to the Right Step by Step,* N.Y. TIMES (June 27, 2013), http://www.nytimes.com/2013/06/28/us/politics/roberts-plays-a-long-game.html?pagewanted=all&_r=0 ("The more meaningful way to look at the court is as a movie, one starring Chief Justice John G. Roberts Jr. as a canny strategist with a tough side, and his eyes on the horizon. He is just 58 and is likely to lead the court for another two decades or more.");

both the left and the right, as Professor Tara Smith has argued, the political ubiquity of charges that minimalism can be and is deployed in "bad faith" may indicate a broader problem with the doctrine—namely that, while minimalism is founded on broad principles, the doctrine, at bottom, "lacks a definite identity," resulting in a failure "either to discipline or to guide its would-be practitioners."[220]

Criticism of the Avoidance Canon

The seventh rule of *Ashwander*—that a court should construe a statute to avoid a construction that raises constitutional problems[221]—has generated significant criticism, as well. First, legal scholars and jurists alike have questioned whether adherence to the constitutional avoidance canon is compatible with the central "objective" of statutory construction: to give effect to the intent of Congress.[222] Critics have argued that it is unrealistic to assume that Congress, in enacting a particular statute, both contemplated a reading of the law that would raise constitutional problems *and* wished to not test the limits of the potential constitutional issue.[223] In this sense, a court, in avoiding a construction of a statute that raises grave constitutional doubts, may adopt an interpretation of a law wholly unintended by the legislature that enacted the law.[224] As a result, the avoidance canon can lead to undemocratic results and can undermine its role as a "vehicle of judicial restraint."[225] For example, as Professor John Manning has argued, if a court misconstrues a statute using the avoidance canon, the interpretation of the statute will remain in place if either house of Congress or the President prefers the court's interpretation, "enshrin[ing] a result that could not have been adopted *ex ante*."[226] Such a criticism of the avoidance canon was provided by Justice Scalia in his concurring opinion in *Bond,* where he accused the majority of the Court of "performing Congress's" job by "rewrit[ing]" the CWCIA, even though—in Scalia's view—"it [was] clear beyond doubt that [the Act] covers what Bond did."[227]

Second, the avoidance canon has been criticized on the grounds that in avoiding to adopt a construction of a statute that raises constitutional doubts, the court must make some sort of pronouncement on a constitutional norm, defeating the entire purpose of the canon as a means toward avoiding answering broad constitutional questions. In this vein, Judge Richard Posner has argued that the avoidance canon's "practical effect" is to enlarge the reach of constitutional law to prevent Congress from legislating in an area that has the mere *potential* to raise serious constitutional questions, "creat[ing] a judge-made 'penumbra' that has much the same prohibitory effect" as a ruling on the underlying constitutional question itself.[228] This "penumbra" effect can

---

[220] *See* Tara Smith, *Reckless Caution: The Perils of Judicial Minimalism,* 5 NYU J.L. & LIBERTY 347, 352 (2010).

[221] 297 U.S. at 348 (Brandeis, J., concurring) ("When the validity of an act of the Congress is drawn in question, and even if a serious doubt of constitutionality is raised, it is a cardinal principle that this Court will first ascertain whether a construction of the statute is fairly possible by which the question may be avoided.").

[222] Kirtsaeng v. John Wiley & Sons, Inc., 133 S. Ct. 1351, 1390 (2013).

[223] *See* William K. Kelley, *Avoiding Constitutional Questions as a Three-Branch Problem,* 86 CORNELL L. REV. 831, 846-60 (2001).

[224] *See* John F. Manning, *The Nondelegation Doctrine as a Canon of Avoidance,* 2000 SUP. CT. REV. 223, 254-55 (2000).

[225] *See* Frederick Schauer, *Ashwander Revisited,* 1995 Sup. Ct. Rev. 71, 98 (1995) (arguing that the avoidance canon permits judges to "substitute their judgment for that of Congress.").

[226] *Id.* at 255.

[227] 134 S. Ct. at 2094 (Scalia, J., concurring).

[228] *See* Richard Posner, *Statutory Interpretation—in the Classroom and in the Courtroom,* U. CHI. L. REV. 800, 816 (continued...)

potentially be seen in Chief Justice Roberts's majority opinion in *Bond*. The *Bond* ruling, while narrow in the sense that it only reached the statutory question posed by the case, is broad in the language it uses, stating that federal laws that criminalize purely local acts "would fundamentally upset the Constitution's balance between national and local power" and would "mark a dramatic departure from that constitutional structure and a serious reallocation of criminal law enforcement authority between the Federal Government and the States."[229] The net result of the *Bond* decision, therefore, is that the Court was able to avoid the constitutional question regarding the scope of the treaty power by making arguably broad pronouncements on Congress's power to enact laws that criminalize local activity, resulting in *Bond* being a case with potentially broad import for constitutional law.[230]

Conclusion

Regardless of the relative merits of constitutional avoidance as a judicial strategy and philosophy, the doctrine of constitutional avoidance appears to have a broad following at the Supreme Court, as demonstrated by the recent terms of the Roberts Court.[231] And the continued viability of the constitutional avoidance doctrine could have significant implications for Congress. In a world with increasing gridlock in Congress, the temptation may be for the legislative branch to draft legislation in a broad, and perhaps vague, manner or wholly ignore major legal questions, with the hopes that the unelected judiciary can help resolve the most pressing legal issues facing the country.[232] This temptation may be especially pronounced with respect to major questions of constitutional law, such as whether the Constitution protects the concept of marriage equality or the limits the Fourth Amendment provides on the ability of the President to conduct foreign intelligence gathering. Nearly 20 years ago, Senator Robert Byrd echoed these concerns during the midst of debate over the drafting of the line-item veto:

> Why are we trying to pass a bill that raises such serious and substantial constitutional questions? We should be resolving those questions on our own. All of us take an oath of office to support and defend the Constitution. During the process of considering a bill, it is our duty to identify—and correct—constitutional problems. We cannot correct these here because we cannot amend the conference report. It is irresponsible to simply punt to the courts, hoping that the judiciary will somehow catch our mistakes.[233]

To the extent Congress "punts" to the Court on an issue of constitutional importance, the constitutional avoidance doctrines raises the possibility that the Court may send the "political football" back to the democratic arena and force the political branches to resolve major constitutional questions on their own. In this sense, the avoidance doctrine may be a means of reinforcing and correcting congressional intransigence on major legal issues, potentially casting

---

(...continued)

(1983).

[229] 134 S. Ct. at 2093-94.

[230] *See* CRS Report WSLG961, *Avoiding the Issue: The Constitutional Avoidance Doctrine and Bond v. United States,* by Andrew Nolan.

[231] *See supra* "The Roberts Court and the Ashwander Doctrine."

[232] *See* Michael J. Teter, *Congressional Gridlock's Threat to Separation of Powers,* 2013 WIS. L. REV. 1097, 1156 (2013).

[233] *See* 142 Cong. Rec. S. 6514 (1996) (statement of Sen. Byrd).

into doubt Alexis de Tocqueville's famous observation that "Scarcely any political question arises in the United States that is not resolved, sooner or later, into a judicial question."[234]

At the same time, as demonstrated by the criticisms of the avoidance doctrine and the Court's willingness to answer major constitutional questions, the *Ashwander* doctrine often does not operate as a comprehensive or cohesive theory. More broadly, the Roberts Court "cannot simply avoid answering difficult moral, social, and political questions altogether," and the High Court may indeed find it conducive to its role in government to provide clarity with respect to certain questions of constitutional law.[235] As a result, the extent to which the federal judiciary ignores the constitutional avoidance doctrine will necessarily dictate Congress's co-equal role in interpreting the Constitution and will, more broadly, animate the extent of dialogue amongst the political branches on matters of constitutional law. In turn, the constitutional avoidance doctrine necessarily becomes the starting point by which the federal judiciary chooses to set forth the chief constitutional rules that police every action of Congress, making the doctrine potentially fundamental to understanding the roles of the judiciary and the political branches in the federal tripartite system of government.

Author Contact Information

Andrew Nolan
Legislative Attorney
anolan@crs.loc.gov, 7-0602

---

[234] *See* Alexis de Tocqueville, DEMOCRACY IN AMERICA, 261 (Henry Reeve trans., 1838).

[235] *See* Henry T. Scott, *Burkean Minimalism and the Roberts Court's Docket,* 6 GEO. J.L. & PUB. POL'Y 753, 778 (2008).

www.ingramcontent.com/pod-product-compliance
Lightning Source LLC
Chambersburg PA
CBHW080748290526
45790CB00008B/3367